THURROCK
PAST & PRESENT

Above: The *Gull* lightship at Grays riverside in the 1950s. It was a clubhouse for the Yacht Club for some time. *(AC)*

Left: The *Gull*'s resting place has been Grays waterfront for many years. Open to the elements and a victim of vandalism, it is likely to disintegrate. It is seen here in 2002 after it was damaged by arson. A restored vessel would make a perfect symbol for the new Grays. *(KL)*

THURROCK PAST & PRESENT

BRIAN EVANS

WHSmith

First published in the United Kingdom in 2002 by
Sutton Publishing Limited exclusively for
WHSmith, Greenbridge Road, Swindon SN3 3LD

British Library Cataloguing in Publication Data
A catalogue record for this book is available from the British Library.

ISBN 0-7509-3110-8

Illustrations

Front endpaper: Grays High Street in about 1912 with only one delivery cart with its horse in front waiting by the kerb on the left. *(AC)*
Back endpaper: View along Grays High Street's western side, 2002. *(BE)*
Half title page: An early twentieth-century drawing of Tilbury Fort seen from the river before the new sea wall was built. *(AC)*
Title page: Grays level crossing, 2002. Now it is only open to pedestrians, but before a new bridge crossing was built further east, traffic and pedestrians mingled when the gates opened. *(BE)*

Typeset in 11/14pt Photina and produced by
Sutton Publishing Limited, Phoenix Mill,
Thrupp, Stroud, Gloucestershire GL5 2BU.
Printed and bound in England by
J.H. Haynes & Co. Ltd, Sparkford.

Contents

The sign says Machine Bakery, a favourite description in the early twentieth century, but the shop appears to sell cigarettes and many other items with a prominent advert for Grays' three cinemas. W.C. Day is the licensee mentioned above the door. *(TMS)*

Introduction

Thurrock is an area of amazing diversity. For many centuries it was off the beaten track and only the road from London to the port at Tilbury connected it with the outside world. This was not a good route by later standards, but it was kept in a state of tolerable repair because of its importance to state officials. In addition, there was a road from the hinterland of Essex which ran from Chelmsford down to the waterside at Tilbury; many times over the centuries it was roundly condemned as the most awful in the kingdom.

What a desolate shore this Thameside area of marshes and low-lying fields must have presented to a traveller journeying across or along the Thames in the inclement seasons of earlier centuries. The starkness of the landscape was especially marked when compared with the beautiful mirage rising out of the mists on the Kent bank opposite – the noble town of Gravesend. However, there were advantages to the site, partly stemming from its very isolation. From its origins in the Coldharbour – the first crude shelter established by early man – the site at Tilbury riverside has developed beyond recognition. Huge ships tower above the landing stage alongside smaller vessels, including preserved sailing barges, which were once a common sight here, and pleasure boats and ferries. Yet looking back towards the north and east there is still a glimpse of the remoteness that stretches back into the distant past.

Tilbury, then, was a key to the Thurrock area. Small agricultural villages with their surrounding acres of fields ran back from the riverfront north, west and east for mile after mile. For centuries they remained only marginally altered by outside influences and political upheavals. A famous exception to the customary isolation occurred at Fobbing, 3 miles east of Stanford-le-Hope, where subjugated farmworkers rose up to join the Peasants' Revolt of 1381. Some of them were executed when the uprising was suppressed. The whole story is told in H. Fagan's book *Nine Days That Shook England.*

To the west of Tilbury grew the present centre of the district properly known as Grays Thurrock. The curious second part of this name is apparently derived from a Saxon word meaning the area in the bottom of a boat where waterborne debris collects. The relevance of the word to Grays lies in the fact that the settlement sits at a deep bend in the river where silt and flood-carried flotsam and jetsam are deposited. In fact the Saxons founded not just Thurrock but a string of settlements along the river, including Mucking, Rainham, Dagenham and Barking. Because the area inland from here was largely marsh and woodland, the villages were reached mostly by water.

After the Norman Conquest the little rural manor known as Turruc had a population of only twenty-eight. The more familiar part of its name originated when the land was

The *Great Eastern* paddle- and screw-driven ship built at Millwall in 1858 and here seen off Purfleet in the nineteenth century when it was the largest vessel of its kind in the world. *(AC)*

granted to Henry de Grai in 1195. This lord had come with William from Graye in Normandy. The town, which was to become a little port, already had a history of occupation by man dating back to the Paleolithic or Old Stone Age through to the Roman era. Bronze Age finds have been especially significant, and Roman artefacts and burials suggest there was a settlement of some substance here in that era as well. The medieval community flourished and spread like a ribbon along the old High Street, linking the waterfront with the old road from Purfleet to West Tilbury – which eventually became London Road and Orsett Road. However, evidence shows that the area which was built on only reached as far as Grays church, where a market is shown on the 1777 Chapman and André map of Essex.

Substantial changes came to the town and to West Thurrock, South Stifford, Purfleet and the riverside areas to the east with the birth of the area's own industrial revolution. Early signs of this development were manifest in the growth of the extractive industries. Chalk quarrying on a bigger scale than the basic pits found in outcrops at Grays, Stifford and Little Thurrock began as early as 1688. But the new focus was on quarrying chalk for lime burning. The lord of the manor, William Palmer, leased a pit and two limekilns close to his house to a Kentish man, John Fookes of Greenwich, who knew all about processing chalk. This pit was still being worked in 1787 when the proprietor was James

Theobald, a famous entrepreneurial name in the district. (The Theobald Arms public house still exists down towards the river.) Theobald was spurred on by his agent to build a new kiln and increase output to compete with the neighbouring pit of another famous local businessman, Zachariah Button.

The chalk trade increased as more uses were found for the product in building and other industries. The chalk pits in Grays (the Titan pit behind the present library, museum and theatre can still be seen) and to the west were linked to wharves on the Thames bank by tramways which crossed the east–west road through the town. They contributed to Grays' unique geography in the nineteenth century and, along with the many Nonconformist chapels, made it resemble the towns of northern England rather than those of the south. Into the twentieth century many industrial railways crossed the road to access the cement and other industries which migrated to the Thames bank. These businesses found the riverside location ideal for bringing goods in and taking out their raw and finished materials.

Purfleet at the western end of Thurrock also displays a unique geography, a mix of man's productive inroads, government intervention and nature's bounty. The presence of

Items from Thurrock brewery and taverns at the museum in Orsett Road, Grays, 2002. *(KL)*

chalk cliffs and outcrops enticed various entrepreneurs to the area from at least the 1550s up to about 1850. The quarry moved eastwards from its original starting point at the Mar Dyke to Beacon Hill, becoming a large-scale enterprise as it developed. There were limeworks on the site which, via the Thames, had ready natural access to important markets. When the railway arrived it was able to take a path through the huge scar that resulted from the old workings.

In time the old pits north of the railway grew a cloak of trees and greenery, and in the latter part of the nineteenth century a bridge over the line gave access to the Botany Gardens; the old pits had become the destination for thousands of day-trippers. Together with the Royal Hotel, the nearby tea-gardens and the superb Thames views, the gardens made Purfleet a mecca for Sunday outings, often the only day of the week a working family had available for pleasure.

The Whitbread family owned the quarries up to their closure in the 1840s and retained an estate north of the railway until 1920. They left a legacy of buildings, cottages, a

The new museum's built-in case displays objects from local retail businesses of an earlier time. There is a timepiece from A.W. Boatman, a plate from the Grays Co-operative Society and early record sleeves from various retailers. *(KL)*

A children's party to celebrate the silver jubilee of King George V and Queen Mary, Grays, 1935. *(TMS)*

school and a chapel, some of which still remain. Unfortunately the sale of the estate enabled industries that were already established to the east on the West Thurrock marshes to expand into the old village and also to take over all the surviving open space along the riverside. The development took away much of the charm and quaintness of this unusual location. A green open space above the Royal Hotel provides a view over the river today and there is a substantial housing development rising below – two of the latest changes to affect this Thurrock outpost.

Last but not least, it must be mentioned that this 'village' once housed the government's powder magazines. They were built here under an Act of Parliament of 1759. The people of Greenwich, the magazines' previous location, wanted the gunpowder moved. A new site at a safer distance from a large centre of population was sought and the powers that be chose Purfleet. The village was still small at the time and its inhabitants were powerless to alter the official verdict. The new magazines were built to as secure a pattern as contemporary scientific knowledge could devise, but later press commentators in the nineteenth century wrote sensational accounts about the likelihood of an explosion and speculated about the size of the area that would be devastated. In the event the stores survived without serious mishap, serving all British military units up to about 1950. Their final closure came in 1962 and most of the stores and other buildings made way for a housing estate in the 1970s. Magazine No. 5, together with the Copper Hoop store, the attractive Clock Tower and a section of the Inner Sanctum Wall, has been conserved. It is within these heritage surroundings that the Purfleet Heritage & Military Centre has established informative displays, open to the public on most Sundays and certain Saturdays during the year.

In Grays, the library, museum and theatre building in Orsett Road has a wealth of historical displays and information on all aspects of Thurrock's diverse heritage. The museum is a vital part of the local community and is involved in many activities, such as history walks and lectures. There is also a local history department in the library section, preserving the past of this area which is still changing every year.

Brian Evans, 2002

Purfleet Garrison Clock Tower, a surviving relic of the gunpowder magazine complex. *(KL)*

Industry Then & Now

A worked-out mineral pit used as camp for German prisoners during the First World War. The abundance of chalk and other mineral workings in use in the nineteenth and early twentieth centuries, and even before that in some locations, has left many scars, some of which are now being ingeniously reused. In West Thurrock the M25 approaches and leaves the river crossings on a remaining chalk ridge which can be seen from the London Road. Lakeside Shopping Centre is built in a huge pit and Chafford Hundred is gradually covering other worked-out quarries with houses. *(TLS)*

The Purfleet cliffs were some of the earliest in the district to be quarried, leaving these islands towering above the landscape. Note the wagons which still hauled the chalk in about 1910. The islands have mostly now gone. *(AC)*

Sketch of the type of wagon used to convey chalk in 1805. There had been very little change in the design by 1910 (*see above*). *(AC)*

Chalk, lime and cement industries implements on display at Thurrock Museum, Orsett Road. *(KL)*

The domes of Lakeside seen from the rim of a former pit. *(BE)*

The Titan pit at Grays Quarries, *c.* 1904. *(AC)*

The entrance to the Titan pit at Grays today. The vegetation hosts a wide variety of wildlife. *(KL)*

The last of the brickworks, Little Thurrock, late nineteenth century. Digging out the brickearth and converting it into bricks was tiring physical labour, and meant long hours for the workmen. During the summer workers often toiled from 4.30 am to 8 pm. There was a beershop nearby to offer a soothing end to the day, and perhaps inevitably drunkeness was rife among the workmen. *(TLS)*

The works office today overlooking the Whitehall Lane pit which houses a host of light industrial buildings. Note the ornate use of many different types of bricks in the structure. *(BE)*

A Thames barge under way – a common sight off Grays when the town was home for one of the largest fleets afloat. *(AC)*

The Thames barge *Thistle* moves away under power from Tilbury landing stage to make room for a cruise vessel, 30 June 2002. *(BE)*

The Grays Co-operative Society Wharf, c. 1915. It was a vital link in the society's chain of supply and distribution. *(AC)*

A yacht off Grays promenade, 2002. This view was not visible to the public until the recent construction of a promenade and new housing behind. This replaced the old wharfside industries that were hidden away behind wooden fences lining the narrow footpath inland. *(BE)*

When the horse was king in Thurrock. A two-horse plough is driven in the old way at Fobbing in the early years of the twentieth century. *(TMS)*

The horses have gone but some reminders of the old rural ways survive. The windmill at Baker Street has been restored and is seen here in 2002. The steam mill buildings have been made into a house. *(KL)*

Mr Osborne, Grays blacksmith, on the right. His was a busy enterprise in the days of universal horse propulsion. *(OF)*

The Forge at Horndon-on-the-Hill employs three generations in 2002. Here we see Alan Theobald (left) and John Clout, who work at the old trade with only a few new methods. John's uncle, David Clout, was out on the road working when this picture was taken. *(KL)*

This photograph of Seabrooke's Brewery (Grays) staff was taken in 1929, the year the brewery closed. Thurrock Museum is attempting to record all the names of the people shown. A display in the museum's foyer shows those traced so far. *(AC)*

The Bull, Corringham. The pub's frontage has been preserved. Many of Seabrooke's public houses would have been like this historic weatherboarded inn. Since the brewery's closure most have been replaced by modern buildings. *(BE)*

These houses now fill the site once occupied by Seabrooke's brewery at the bottom of Bridge Road, Grays. *(BE)*

A reminder of the past. This sculpture of a Thames sailing barge faces the level crossing at Grays. On the side of the base is an evocative poem by T.S. Eliot. *(KL)*

The original Kollergang pulping machines at Thames Board Mills (TBM) and the interior of the original mill in 1888. In the 1880s an enterprising Belgian called Maurice Cartiaux brought over part of the framework of the buildings set up for the Antwerp Exhibition and set it up at Purfleet to make strawboard from waste straw. He is the second figure from the left in the drawing (which is based directly on an early photograph). The original name of the works was the St Louis Park Mills. *(AC)*

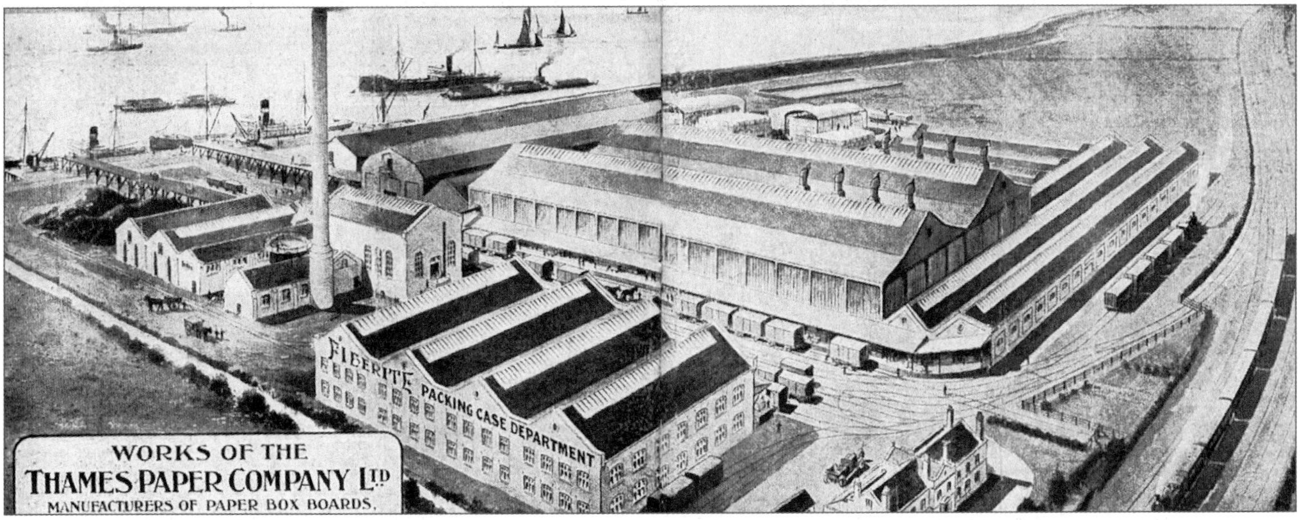

Above: The works as they looked in about 1910. *(AC)*

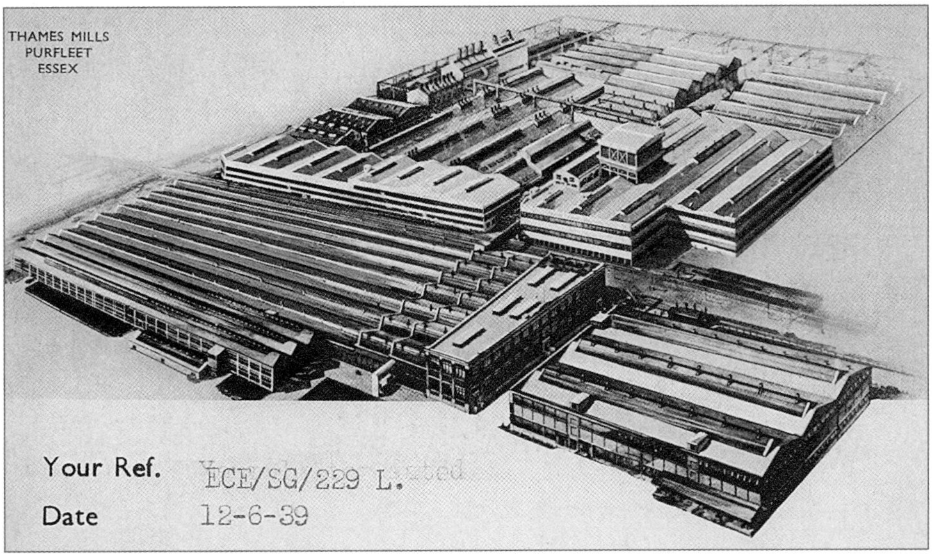

A postcard used for correspondence shows the mills in the 1930s. *(AC)*

DANGER

On 13 February 1953 the young Queen Elizabeth visited TBM's Purfleet works as part of her tour of flooded Thameside areas. Mr G. Johnstone accompanied her around the factory. *(TBM)*

The impressive dockside cranes of Thames Board Mills, *c.* 1928. The development of industry along the Thurrock Thameside from the late nineteenth century is a story of impressive energies focused on finding the best way to manufacture and distribute the goods vital to 'modern' lifestyles. Thames Mills, for instance, produced boxes carrying the brand names of the newly advertised products that came in with the twentieth century and replaced bagged-on-purchase items. *(AC)*

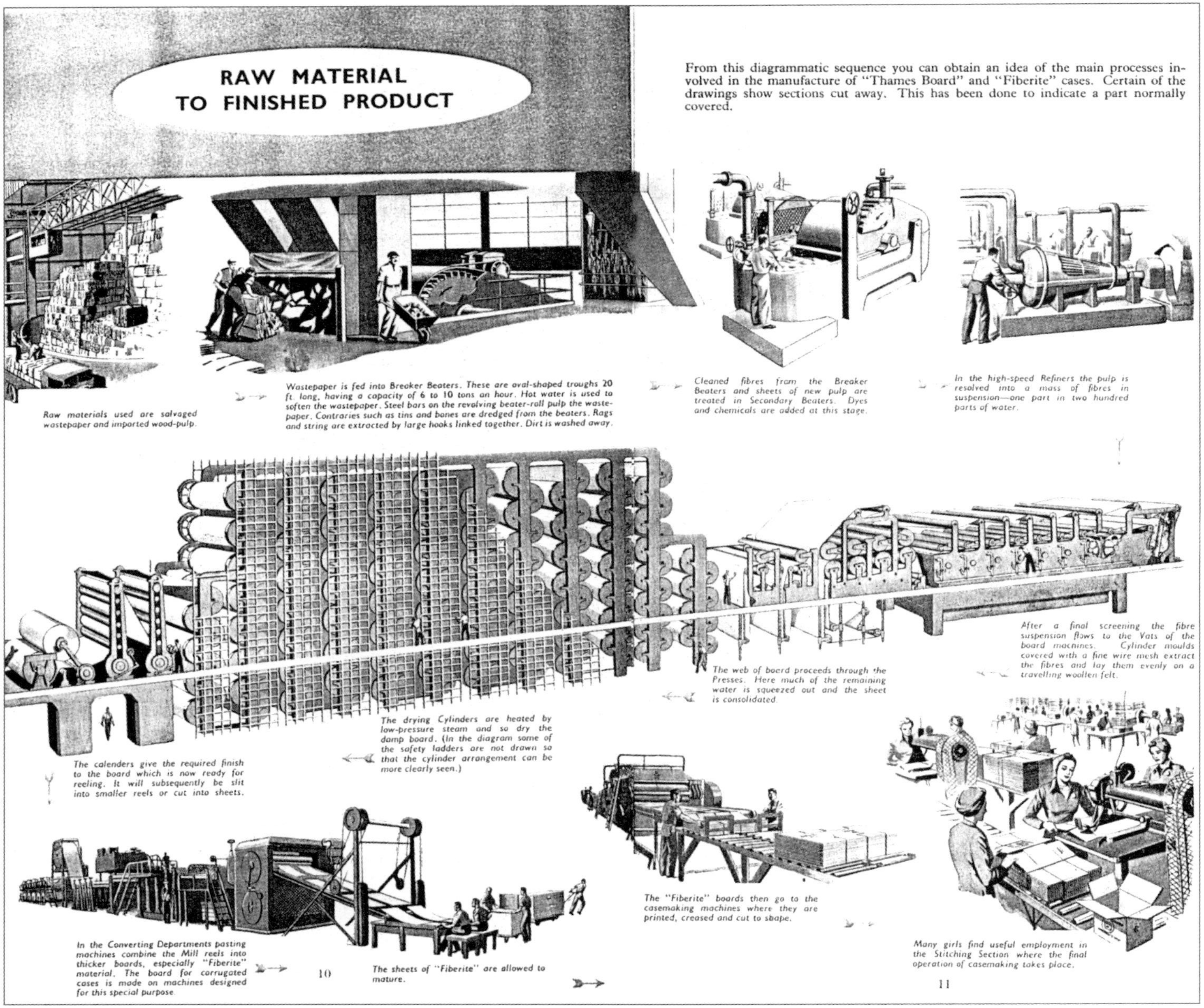

The processes involved in the manufacture of Thames Board and 'Fiberite' cases in the 1950s. *(TBM)*

TBM, 1954. The office block is in the foreground and beyond is the St Andrew's cross pattern of the Rest Garden. The solid and corrugated converting factories lie on the left and right of Mill Road which runs down the centre of the picture. Beyond the railway is the range of mill buildings with the smoking stacks of the power house at the top of the picture. *(TBM)*

Modern offices at Thames Board Mills, *c.* 1960. There were fewer cars when this photograph was taken but little else has changed here since then. *(AC)*

The Bata shoe factory, 1930s. Not only a factory but a whole community rose up on the bleak East Tilbury landscape. Note the Auto Service station on the right (petrol, oil, tyres, batteries and repairs). *(AC)*

The Bata factory area is now known as Thames Industrial Park and houses a variety of enterprises with a residual Bata presence. The original Bata village community, built on lonely fields, included a welfare scheme, sports and social club, cinema, hotel with a catering/dining hall for 1,000 and separate accommodation for single employees, social hall, housing estate, children's playground, shopping facilities, farm and dairy, primary school and weekly newspaper. *(BE)*

Ambrose Bros mineral water factory in Grays used this delivery lorry in the early twentieth century. A proud Mr Ambrose stands in front with his son and two workers. *(TMS)*

A modern lorry passes along Orsett Road, Grays, 2002. *(AC)*

Thames Haven cylinder storage tanks, 1920s. The site is in the parish of Corringham and developed in the late nineteenth and early twentieth centuries. The original plan was for a dock area with railway links, but the building of Tilbury Docks in 1886 put an end to this scheme. It later became one of the largest independent oil reservoirs in Europe. *(AC)*

A similar storage tank farm at Purfleet, 2002. *(AC)*

Aerial view of Ciment Fondu's works at West Thurrock at the end of the Second World War. *(AC)*

Lakeside now covers a large former industrial pit area in West Thurrock on the other side of the M25 to the Ciment Fondu site. This is the entrance to the shopping centre from the bus station. *(BE)*

The dairy and multiplex rollers at Van Den Berghs & Jurgens works, 1950s. Stork margarine was produced here and became a top brand in postwar Britain. The butter substitute was invented in 1889 by the French chemist Hippolyte Mege-Mouries. Van den Berghs and Jurgens were originally two separate margarine manufacturers who were invited to begin margarine production in this country by the government during the First World War. *(AC)*

The post-Second World War dominance of Stork margarine has been challenged in recent years. Stork is now produced primarily for baking, while Van Den Berghs make many new spreads and butter substitutes, such as Flora, Olivio, I Can't Believe It's Not Butter and Delight.

At the Centre

A sunny day at the north end of Grays High Street, 1903. There was no traffic problem in the early twentieth century, except the danger of colliding with other people in the middle of the road! By this time nearly all the old houses had gained shopfronts. A delivery cart on the far right advertises the Lipton Tea Company and above it a shop board says 'Furnish. Ready Cash. Easy Terms'. Moving left we see Bell's Stores and Charles Mitcham, drapers. The Queen's Hall lies in the shadow on the left. The road is devoid of signs and all the clutter of today's world. *(AC)*

Looking down the High Street from the level crossing you were in no danger of being run down by vehicles in 1907. Crown Road with its one-way traffic did not exist until the mid-1990s. The London & Provincial Bank on the right became Barclays and was still flourishing into the 1960s and beyond. However, it and a signal-box adjacent to the crossing gates were later pulled down to create room for the road. Note on the left Walker's ironmongery displaying a wide range of products on the pavement. *(BE)*

Today Crown Road runs in the foreground next to the level crossing (which is out of view). Once again pedestrians can stroll about the High Street unhindered because traffic has been banned since the mid-1990s. *(AC)*

Grays Beach was created through the inspiration of the local council which brought large amounts of sand to the foreshore. This picture was taken in 1905, not long after the beach was created. There was a paddling pool but little else in the way of structures until recent times. *(AC)*

Grays Beach paddling pool, remodelled like the rest of the beach area which now contains a host of other adventure playground features to keep modern children happy. Behind the trees the shore has now been developed for industrial use. *(BE)*

A classic photograph of the river end of High Street, *c.* 1906. Two boys on the left have hoops and a wide range of adult onlookers stand outside the Anchor & Hope pub (125 High Street, James Broyd, beer retailer) on the right. Every kind of business crowded this end of the street at this time, but nautical interests were evident. Charles Thwaites was a shipsmith at no. 43 and there was also a marine store dealer. A master mariner lived in New Road nearby. Some of the men in the picture were probably involved with the sailing barge fleet based in Grays. *(AC)*

The same High Street site today. The area has been opened out with grass verges on either side leading to high-rise buildings and down to the Thames. The buildings in the distance towards the church were rebuilt more than once in the later twentieth century. *(BE)*

The Theobald Arms in Grays today. Apart from the modern street furniture and a few other touches this could be an old photograph. The pub was part of the considerable estates of James Theobald MP who fell under a railway train at Romford Station in 1894. What a tale this inn could tell if it could speak. It sits on the former waterfront and much of the history of Grays as a port and home of a Thames barge fleet owned by E.J. & W. Goldsmith would have been told within these walls. At its peak the Goldsmith enterprise had 140 vessels trading around the coast of Britain. *(KL)*

Near the waterfront opposite the Theobald Arms is this old bargemaster's house, now the home of Pier Lodge Nursery. *(KL)*

The northernmost section of the High Street, looking towards the level crossing, 1912. A Lipton's delivery tricycle sits at the kerb. On the right is James Nelson & Sons, butchers, at no 6. The International Stores at no. 8 are evidence of national multiple traders moving in. In the distance a large sign proclaims 'Garage' – a sign of times to come, and at this stage only meaning a trader who could order a motor vehicle for prospective customers and provide some basic servicing. *(AC)*

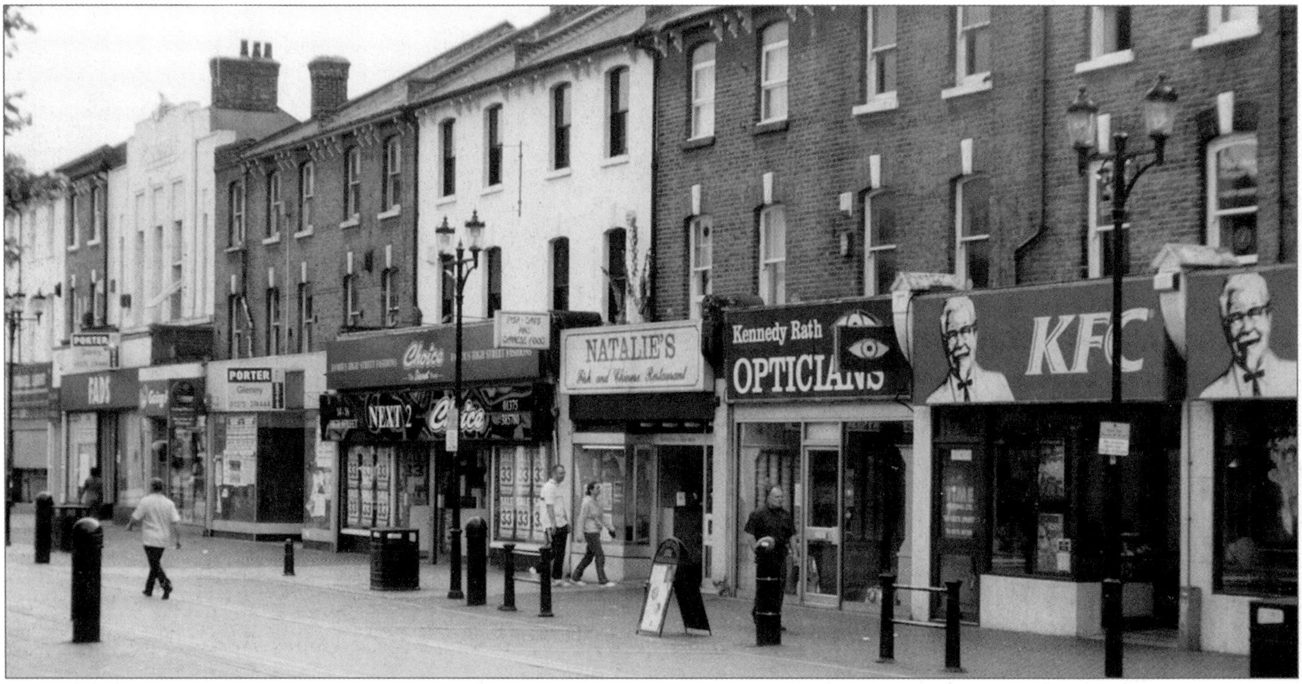

The shops in this part of the High Street in 2002 provide outlets for modern preoccupations such as fast food and personal appearance, though several were empty when this picture was taken. *(BE)*

The level crossing from the south. One of the most famous Grays scenes, this has changed gradually over the years since this photograph was taken in about 1924. The railway café on the left (Charles H. Bilton proprietor) also offered baths, a garage and a hotel, though how this was possible in the limited space is a puzzle. Motor vehicles were beginning to grow in number in the High Street by this time. *(AC)*

The crossing, 2002. The fencing and pavement have been augmented to provide for pedestrian access only. A parking bay for cars has been created. Out of sight on the left are the latest in a long line of establishments continuing the tradition of cafés and takeaways. *(BE)*

Joyes of New Road, Grays, early 1900s. A long-established department store, Joyes had a fabrics and materials section with no fewer than four staff. The long serving counter and strategically placed chairs for customers who were always right were typical of the period. *(AC)*

Joyes continued to trade through the twentieth century. Here is an advertisement from 1953. Once a prosperous shopping street, New Road now consists mainly of the Civic Centre. *(AC)*

The calm face of shopping on the original New Road, looking from Grays Church end, *c.* 1905. Joyes' premises are on the right and the famous Horncastle's store on the left. *(AC)*

In 2002 all that is left of the shops is a takeaway, advice centre and café. Beyond looms the impressive pile of the modern Thurrock Council offices. *(BE)*

A busy riverside scene on the Grays waterfront including a Thames barge, 1960s. The skyline had become very industrial by this time. *(TMS)*

Postwar high-rise buildings form a backdrop to sailing vessels parked behind the sea wall at Grays in 2002. *(KL)*

The original Wharf Hotel, 1950s. At this time it was completely surrounded by maritime concerns and was rather cut off from Grays proper. (AC)

A new housing area has now been built over the old Thameside shoreline of shipbreaking and small industry and has connected up The Wharf rather impressively with the main town. The pub attracts custom from the new residents and from outsiders in 2002. Some of the new and interesting designs for the housing scheme can be seen beyond The Wharf. *(BE)*

Wards Yard, Grays Wharf, where this old submarine was being broken up in 1930, lay behind the old creosoted railway sleeper fence which separated the footpath to The Wharf pub from the various riverside yards and industrial activities. *(AC)*

Today this impressive development of houses lies on the site of the old muddy footpath and untidy yards. It has its own Thameside promenade, opening up panoramic views of the river once denied to the ordinary spectator at this point. *(BE)*

Over the border in Little Thurrock, this is the shop at the junction of College Avenue, Southend Road and Chadwell Road in about 1912. Groups of children straddle the pavement and the carriageway, quite unconcerned for their safety. Mrs Emily Watson was the shopkeeper running a grocery; she also sold stamps. On the opposite side of the road was a surgical bootmaker called Arthur Meudham who ministered to the large number of folk who had foot disablement either through birth or industrial accidents. These problems could not be corrected by an operation. *(AC)*

The view today. The shop doorway has been moved from the corner on to the main frontage and the store advertises its range of goods outside, including videos. Opposite, new premises have been built on a spare corner plot on Chadwell Road. There is now a great deal of traffic and a mini-roundabout. *(BE)*

The Queen's Hotel, 1914. Once Grays' pride and joy, this classy establishment had a number of separate departments – off licence, stores and various bars. This frontage at the bottom of the High Street became more valuable in recent years, suitable for national chain stores and other retailers, and the Queen's relocated to the rear. *(AC)*

The Queen's is now the building with the mini-tower at the centre of this 1999 view of Clarence Road. The bars face a courtyard entrance to the right of the tower so that drinkers can sit outside in good weather – a modern trend following continental practice. *(BE)*

Little Thurrock Broadway, *c.* 1912. The word Broadway is a misnomer – it is not particularly wide! The view is still recognisable today, most of the buildings having survived from its more prosperous heyday. *(AC)*

Today the Broadway displays signs of the times: a mobile phone shop, a Chinese takeaway, a motor spares business, a posh wedding car (on its way to Tilbury?) and an impromptu cabaret performed by a bystander. *(BE)*

River View, Chadwell St Mary, late 1920s or early 1930s. *(AC)*

Terrace of shops at the Cross Keys end of River View, 2002. *(BE)*

Looking up Chadwell Hill, 1920s. The church tower only just looks over the greenery on the right. *(AC)*

This is the interesting house that hides behind the trees in the middle of the picture above (just below the church). *(BE)*

The Cross Keys is in the centre distance in the old view. Here it is in 2002 with agricultural traffic passing. *(BE)*

Orsett Road from the end of the High Street is a playground for children dressed in their Sunday best in this view from the early 1900s. The trees on the hill above the Dell are visible on the horizon. A. Russell's shop (left, with sunblind) was described as a photographers but the window also advertises Boyd organs. Perhaps Mr Russell took this picture. The front gardens of the houses were later removed. *(AC)*

New concepts in shopping and the advent of modern life-styles have dictated the emergence of supermarkets selling a very wide range of goods under one large roof. Morrisons opened in 2002, changing the face of Grays considerably. It occupies part of the old bus station and a new one has been designed between the store and the railway line. The road system has also been redesigned and there will be further regeneration to follow. *(BE)*

Orsett Ascendant

Lieutenant Colonel Francis Whitmore poses by his chauffeur-driven motor at the East Porch of Orsett Hall, *c.* 1912. He revitalised the Orsett Estate from 1896 onwards and served as a justice of the peace for sixty-three years. Whitmore was Lord Lieutenant of Essex from 1936 to 1958 and also Lord of the Manor of Orsett, Little Thurrock, Stifford, Corringham and even North Benfleet. By a strange early local government arrangement, a portion of the distant parish of Stock was a detached part of Orsett. The village is 4 miles north-east of Grays and was the original administrative centre and provider of welfare for the wider district. *(AC)*

Mayors of Essex boroughs and districts and other dignitaries at the Coronation Banquet held by Lord Lieutenant Francis Whitmore at his home, Orsett Hall, on the evening of 26 June 1953. Lady Whitmore is seated in the centre and Sir Francis is on the right. *(AC)*

Orsett Hall in the 1920s, surrounded by parkland and farms. Many new farming methods were tried out on the Orsett Estate in the late nineteenth and twentieth centuries. *(AC)*

Orsett Hall's splendid frontage today. The hall is now a hotel. *(BE)*

A view of the entrance to an extension that provides extra banqueting facilities. *(BE)*

The past preserved in the present. The Pound and Lock-up or Cage at the top of Pound Lane have survived with help of a restoration programme. Most villages have lost these once essential features used to pen stray animals. *(KL)*

A modern archway in Orsett village recreates the arches that were a feature of the village in calm bygone days. *(KL)*

The days of the horse are not quite over as this picture taken in Baker Street on a quiet day shows. *(KL)*

Orsett still has a bus link with Grays but a second route passing through has recently been withdrawn, increasing the need for cars and taxis which could one day overwhelm the traditional quietness of the village. *(KL)*

Birch Cottage, 1913. Older than the Whitmore Arms next door, it consists of a sixteenth-century cross-wing with seventeenth-century additions – making it a substantial structure. *(AC)*

Birch Cottage next to the Whitmore Arms with its wonderful thatched roof has survived intact for centuries. Photographs taken in the early twentieth century, such as the one above, show it looked very similar then, but not quite so well cared for. *(KL)*

A Prince Charles effigy entitled 'A Royal Flush'. A tradition has grown up in the village of displaying costumed scarecrows every year and there is a competition to create the best one. Because 2002 was golden jubilee year, royalty was the theme for the competition. Other effigies included Henry VIII and his six wives, and a guardsman on sentry duty. *(KL)*

Eastern Limits

Billet Road, Stanford-le-Hope, 1920s. It is now slightly less rural. *(AC)*

The old roadsweeper at the end of Corringham Road, Stanford-le-Hope, *c.* 1907. Two horse-drawn delivery vehicles block the road. *(AC)*

The same scene today. Road markings constrain the traffic. Stanford has developed from a village into a township and commuter area. *(BE)*

Terraces of houses line Fetherston Road, Stanford, 1911. Though the houses look urban, the village was still a very quiet place, served by steam trains. *(AC)*

Fetherston Road, ideal for city commuters, 2002. An electrification scheme in the 1950s improved the railway connection between London and south-east Essex. *(BE)*

EVERY PURCHASER BOUND TO BE SUITED. 23

Stanford-le-Hope, Essex.

Having a station on the London, Tilbury, and Southend Railway, six miles from Tilbury Fort and Docks (a great industrial centre), 16 miles South-east from Romford, and 25 miles from the centre of London.

There is a good service of trains to and from the Metropolis, and the return fare is only 2/-, thus bringing the Estate into easy reach of town, and enhancing its value as a Residential Property for City men.

The village of Stanford-le-Hope, situate on Mucking Creek, near Hope Reach, on the Thames, is a clean and go-ahead little place, possessing Shops, Post and Telegraph Offices and Bank.

There is a very interesting old Church there, the chancel being a fine specimen of the Decorated Period of Edward III.

There is a Workmen's Club, Reading Room, and Art and Technical Classes are held at the School.

The soil is light and heavy, subsoil gravel and sand.

"Balstonia" is situate about half mile from the village, having a long frontage to the Southend Road, and consists of 450 acres of excellent well-timbered arable and pasture land, well adapted for development, having very pretty views over a wide expanse of undulating well-wooded country.

A page from Homesteads Ltd's Edwardian brochure, *c.* 1908, describing its suburb of 'Balstonia – about half a mile from Stanford village'. *(AC)*

Properties in the Homesteads development, 2002. Today these older houses have been joined by many newer homes built in the century since the original planning of the suburb. *(AC)*

Central Avenue, Corringham, in the 1930s (above) and today (below). It still has a narrow entrance from Lampitts Hill and the introduction of motor vehicles is one of the few changes. In the old village centre there are more shops than there were in the 1930s and new houses were built after the Second World War. There is a new shopping centre to the north-west of old Corringham. *(AC)*

By the church at Fobbing in the 1950s (above) and 2002 (below). Boats once sailed up a creek close to the village but the water has since receded. *(Above, AC; below, KL)*

One side of West Tilbury village green, *c.* 1926. Even today the green provides the centrepiece for a compact community. *(AC)*

Apart from the cars in the lower picture very little has changed around West Tilbury village green and the King's Head over the last century. *(KL)*

East Tilbury Place, which is a couple of hundred years old, is seen here in a picture from the Essex Field Club archives. This photograph was taken on 8 September 1934. *(AC)*

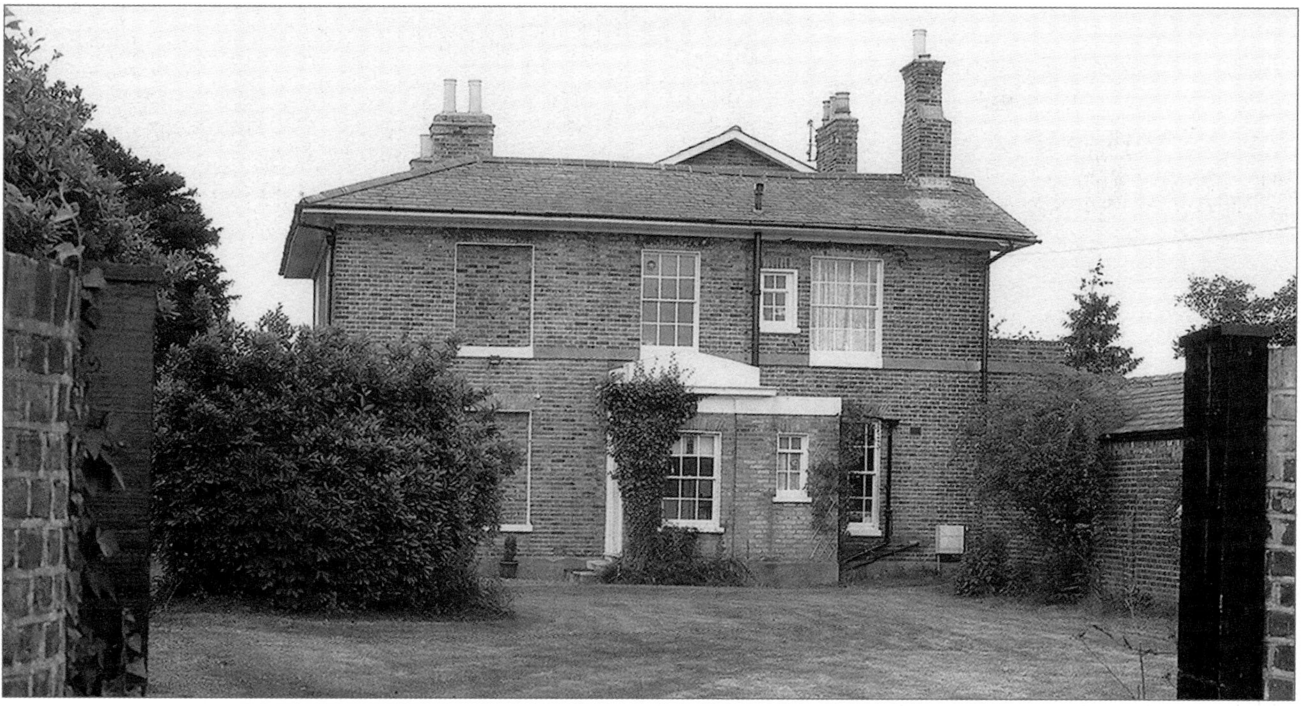

East Tilbury Rectory complements St Catherine's church across the way. The mellow brick building has bricked-up windows reminiscent of the days of window tax avoidance. The bricking up would also keep the house warmer, as it faces the weather heading over the Thames marshes on the side facing the camera. *(KL)*

To come upon this row of shops at Linford in the early twentieth century must have been quite a shock. They were built in the middle of the countryside in the style of a town shopping terrace. *(AC)*

Today the same shops are still a surprise in their location but with some housing development they fit in better. *(KL)*

Tilbury-on-Thames

A sailing barge framed in the hall doorway of the old Tilbury Hotel, 1920s. World travellers, a more exclusive fraternity then, often disembarked from one great liner, stayed a number of nights at the hotel and then re-embarked on another luxury ship for a new destination. The hotel was burned out during an attack by enemy aircraft in 1944. The massive frontage gave a cheerful welcome to passengers returning to England. The town of Tilbury was hidden behind the hotel and the masts and cranes of Tilbury Docks were the only other indication of civilisation on this side of the river. The long terrace, a small part of which can be seen outside the door, was probably the finest viewing platform on the Thames for observing the continuous stream of river vessels. The whole Tilbury area was formerly marsh and merely a southern rural end of Chadwell St Mary parish. The construction of the docks in 1886 led to a rapidly growing population, at first living in makeshift conditions. Tilbury Urban District, set up in 1912, created the basic amenities and infrastructure for a proper town, at the centre of which was Civic Square. *(AC)*

The landing stage at Tilbury, *c.* 1904. Among the early shipping companies to use Tilbury were the Orient Pacific, Maru (Japanese) and the Atlantic Transport Line. In about 1903 the Peninsular & Oriental Steam Navigation Company (P&O) arrived. *(AC)*

The bridge on to the landing stage, 2002. *(BE)*

The *Dunbar Castle* at Tilbury landing stage in 1935, one of the big liners that called here on its way to southern climes. This was the normal mode of transport for world travellers at this time. Only a small but growing number travelled by air. *(AC)*

The Thames sailing barge *Thistle* pulled alongside the landing stage is in the foreground. The massive bulk of the *Astoria* floats beyond. She is one of a new generation of cruise ships. *(BE)*

Loading and unloading a cargo vessel in Tilbury docks, *c.* 1930. *(AC)*

A gigantic container ship berthing on the outside of the docks in 2002, where special cranes await its cargo as the sun begins to set. The size of today's vessels means it is difficult to fit the whole hull into a standard camera lens. *(BE)*

The Tilbury Housing Scheme in 1922. Across a wide empty area the earliest dwellings form the side of a square. In the middle are stacks of bricks. Only set up in 1912 and in existence until 1936, Tilbury Urban District Council rushed to provide decent housing for the growing town. The earliest plans for development were approved in the council's first year. Subsequently, under chairmen A. Brennan (1913–21) and J.F. Feenan (1921–5) the giant scheme was extended. In the course of a decade Tilbury more than doubled its population. During this time the attractive municipal centre known as Civic Square was created. *(AC)*

A glimpse of the shopping parade in Civic Square today (middle) and the edge of the civic buildings (right). There are houses on the far left. *(BE)*

The Tilbury Town Band of 1933/4, apparently photographed by the river bank. Back row, left to right: S. Hills, J. Knight, F. Miller, R. Hayes, W. Mower, G. Mower, F. Chipperfield, R.J. Nicholls, M. Walford, H. Knight, T. Parfrey, E. Harris, P. Knight, G. Sinclair, P. Sanday (new member). Middle row: C. Palmer, N. Miller, T. Carbery, C. Rouse, C. Simmons, F. Miller, E. Martyn. Front row: H. Wright, N. Gray, A. Miller, J. Mansfield. *(BE)*

Below: Very few belong to brass bands these days. In 2002 shopping itself is a hobby and gardening an absorbing pastime – even a serious business. The shops here in Civic Square still look good today. *(BE)*

We do not have a year for this delightful photograph of a Tilbury wedding but the soldier in uniform may indicate a First World War date. *(AC)*

Tilbury working men and three ladies enjoy a pint in the 1950s. The proceeds from exhibiting a whale washed up from the Thames provided money for the first Tilbury Dock Club. A new club was opened in Calcutta Road in 1914. Ever since Tilbury has had a number of social clubs, including an Irish Club opposite Tilbury Town station. *(TMS)*

The carnival pauses at Tilbury Dwellings, *c.* 1904. The Dwellings were the original docks company's solution to housing a large number of manual workers in the 1880s. They consisted of two four-storey blocks and though on this carnival day decorations had brightened them up, they usually had a rather sombre face like housing in big industrial cities – although there is something rather 'Tilbury' and local in their aspect. The Grays Volunteer Artillery lends a martial aspect, setting off the glamour provided by the beauty queen and her retinue. Note the remaining grass bank to the right. *(TMS)*

The site of the dwellings is now absorbed into the busy dock area. It was eventually decided that the dwellings were an inappropriate first view of England for people disembarking ships and travelling on to London. In 1943 the East Block was demolished and the West Block followed in 1962. *(BE)*

Western Approaches

The Beacon experimental lighthouse, Purfleet. Trinity House was responsible for constructing this lighthouse following a decision taken in August 1828. The idea was to use it to carry out experiments with the various types of lamps and reflectors then under consideration, including a French lamp and polyzonal lens. Experiments were also to be made with the illuminants available at the time: whale oil, spermaceti (a wax removed from whales) and seal oil. A quarter of an acre of the high cliff belonging to Mr Whitbread was rented for a nominal sum. Beacon Hill had originally gained its name from the fire that was to be lit there in time of national emergency and may have been used at the time of the Armada, 1588. The lighthouse appears to have been abandoned in the 1870s but was a popular sight for tourists and day-trippers. Today a modern beacon container stands on the open green space above the Royal Hotel. *(AC)*

Cottages in the Hollow, Purfleet, a rather secluded location, *c.* 1912. *(AC)*

The same cottages in 2002. Some development has also taken place around them. *(BE)*

The Royal Hotel, Purfleet, 1920s. Originally called the Bricklayers Arms (1769–1820) and then the Purfleet Tavern and Hotel, its present name was acquired in the 1870s when the Prince of Wales visited. At that time the hotel was well known for its whitebait suppers. *(AC)*

The Royal Hotel today from the inland side. The wilderness below it today makes a picture taken from the Thames frontage, like the one above, more difficulticult. *(BE)*

Soldiers garrisoned in Purfleet protecting the Powder Magazine look out over the Thames below the Royal Hotel in about 1904. *(AC)*

Today their view would be blocked by these smart new apartments known as Harrison's Wharf. After a century when industry appeared to be gaining the upper hand in Purfleet, residential development is fighting back. The heritage of this area certainly gives it a cachet. *(BE)*

The ribbon development of London Road, West Thurrock, *c.* 1912. The nearest house on the left has been converted into William J. Rice's general shop. This is the point west of Mill Lane and the Chase where South Stifford becomes West Thurrock. *(AC)*

The same area of West Thurrock today. The taller white building on the right is the Shant pub. Traffic is fairly continuous these days. *(BE)*

High Street, Aveley, 1920. There was a fashion at the time for shopkeepers to install projecting triangular metal signs announcing the nature of their business to passing traffic. *(AC)*

In 2002 the profile of Aveley's High Street remains similar, but the modern signs are not very visible from this point. *(BE)*

Mill Road, Aveley, 1920s. An old thatched cottage still stood at the High Street corner at this time and there were brick-built homes beyond. This postcard was published by Mr Barker at the village's post office. *(AC)*

Today the left-hand side of Mill Road has been swept clean of houses and a garage/filling station now stands at the corner (out of view). In contrast, the right-hand side of the road has retained its original shape. *(BE)*

The immaculately turned out fire brigade at Purfleet Garrison with military officers standing by. In the early twentieth century the fire hazard posed by the powder storage magazine had not diminished from the eighteenth century when the material was first moved here from Greenwich. But the skill and equipment of the firemen paraded in front of the Commandant's House had improved. All of the main buildings except Magazine No. 5 have now been demolished to make way for a housing estate. A reminder of the former glories is the museum, open on Sundays and some Saturdays in the remaining magazine buildings. *(TMS)*

Charming Churchview Cottage in a recent photograph of the picturesque village street, North Stifford. The parish of Stifford reaches down to the river and the southern part became industrialised in the nineteenth and twentieth centuries. There were chalk pits as well as farms in the area even earlier. *(BE)*

Publicity brochure for new housing in Chafford Hundred between Grays and Lakeside. A large number of developers are converting the old landscape, some of it excavated ground reclaimed by nature. *(AC)*

Northern Heights

Langdon Hills from North Hill, *c.* 1904. This is a favourite high viewpoint for tourists. Only part of the area is in Thurrock but a large part of the district can be seen from above. Langdon, Bulphan, Horndon and South Ockendon are the breezier uplands of Thurrock and have churches of interest; these villages recall old days, old inhabitants and customs of the past. Today Langdon, Bulphan and Horndon are valued for their smallness and isolation. South Ockendon, though well built up to the south, borders open green belt countryside on the north. Thames Chase Forest – a new development intended to give access to a reinvigorated natural landscape – is making progress and providing a new rural destination, particularly for people in the Belhus/Ockendon area. *(AC)*

Gordon Road, a new development for the village of Horndon-on-the Hill in the early twentieth century. *(AC)*

In 2002 Horndon has some new houses and a recently built village hall. While this was being constructed the remains of a tannery from some centuries back were unearthed. One of the vital bus links with the outside world is seen passing through the village. *(KL)*

The northern section of the High Street, Horndon, *c.* 1930. Part of the Swan Inn is on the far right. *(AC)*

The Swan Inn area today. Under the arch is a wonderful panoramic view of the countryside beyond. Inside there is the intimate atmosphere that 'real' locals always acquire. *(KL)*

Mine host and hostess at the Swan Inn, Horndon, July 2002. *(KL)*

Part of Horndon's past – the village pump and post mill, *c.* 1905. Horndon is a village set on a low hilltop, a place which still has immense charm. There is still the kind of community spirit that other places have lost. The church is a gem with several features of particular interest, including the timber supports inside the tower and the carving known as the 'Horndon Beauty'. *(AC)*

Centres for the latest gossip at Horndon-on-the-Hill past and present – The Crown at Langdon Hills in 1920 and the post office today. *(Above, AC; below, KL)*

J. BATES
Mineral Waters
J. BATES
Mineral Waters

West Street, South Ockendon, 1910 (*left*) and 2002 (*above*). The left-hand side of the road is still recognisable but the houses on the right were demolished and postwar housing substituted, although it is hidden behind the trees in this picture. *(AC)*

The school and other buildings in South Ockendon, 1912. Green verges and trees abound. *(AC)*

View over Manor Farm, Bulphan, 1920s. *(AC)*

The farmhouse today. Bulphan still looks out over a wide landscape of farmland – once part of Bulphan Fen. *(BE)*

Moving Forward – Transport Then & Now

An AEC Regal with stylish coachwork operated by the old established Harris Coaches of Grays is used to advertise the business in the mid-twentieth century. Fewer people had their own cars in the 1940s, 1950s and early 1960s and coach travel was popular. The firm then operated from 8 Parker Road. The business today has a booking office in Orsett Road. *(AC)*

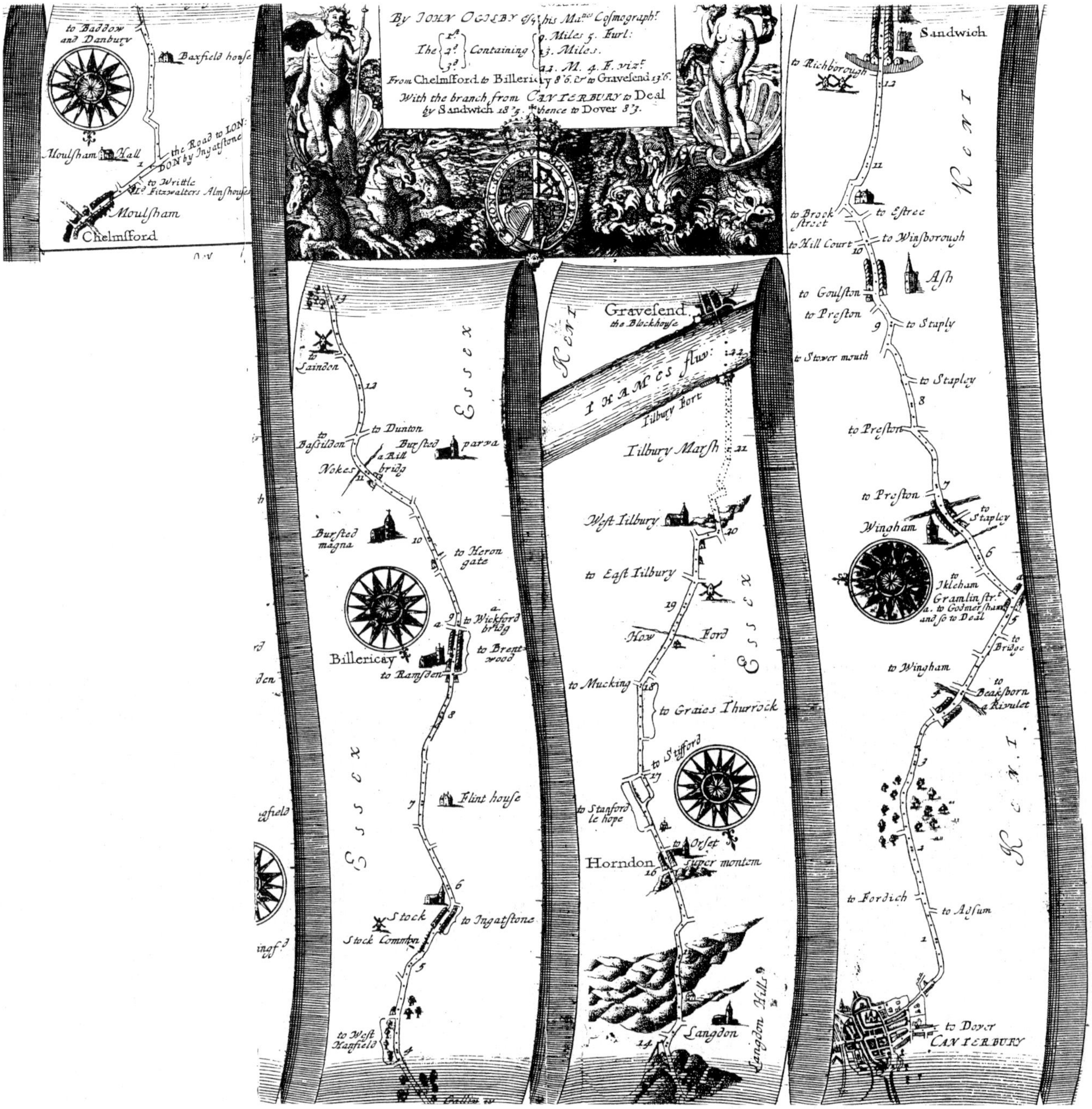

Road maps are not new. This is part of Ogilby's road map of 1675. It shows the route from Chelmsford to Tilbury and into Kent via the Thames. The roads at this time were in an atrocious state, making travel very difficult. Even in 1767 Arthur Young, an Essex-born agricultural writer, made contemptuous comments concerning the road from Billericay to the ferry in his *Six Weeks Tour*: 'A turnpike was much solicited for by some gentlemen to lead from Chelmsford to the Ferry at Tilbury Fort but opposed by the Bruins of the County. Of all the cursed roads which ever disgraced the Kingdom none ever equalled that from Billericay to the King's Head at Tilbury. The ruts are of incredible depth, and I must not forget the chalk wagons, frequently stuck fast till a collection of them are in the same situation, that twenty or thirty horses may be attached to each to draw them out one by one.' Shortly after this the parish roads began to improve. In 1807, forty years after his original outburst, Young credited the by-roads as much improved. *(AC)*

A horse and cart passing the Ship Inn, Little Thurrock (one of the old Hornchurch brewery's pubs), just before the First World War. The ride was still jolting (no rubber tyres) and the horse was still the universal mode of traction, but times were changing and at least the roads were passable. *(AC)*

An amazing transformation – the new Ship Inn today. Behind the exotic flora are outside tables and the horse and cart have been replaced by the ubiquitous motor car. The pub was rebuilt in the twentieth century to serve a new generation who expected interiors to be more inviting. *(BE)*

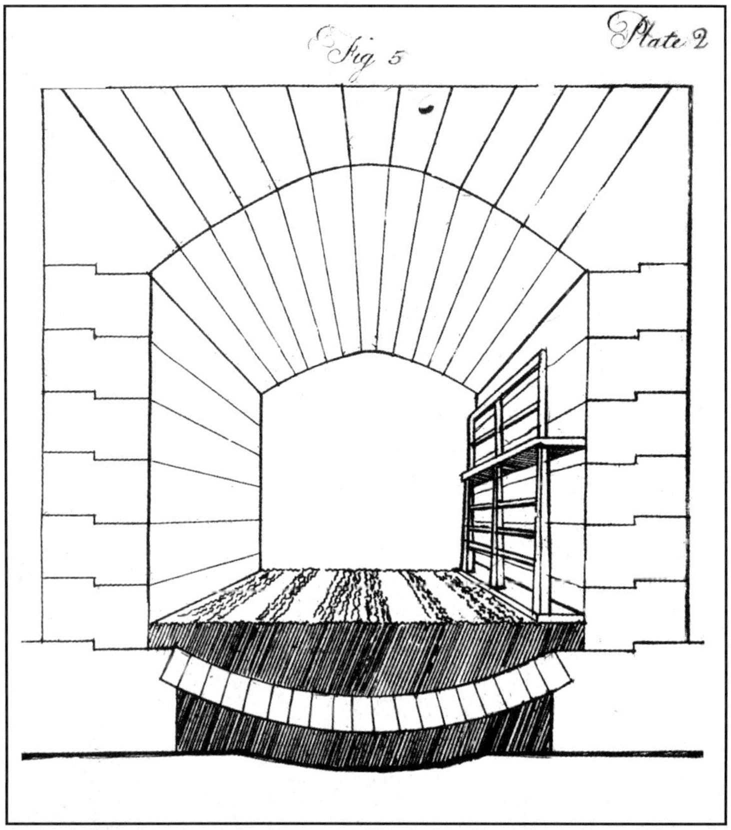

An early plan to build a tunnel under the Thames. As early as 1798 Ralph Dodd, a mining engineer, visited Gravesend with a project for 'a subterranean and subaqueous passage from Gravesend to Tilbury' – that is, a tunnel under the Thames. An Act of Parliament was obtained to set up a company, and work was started on a shaft that reached a depth of 85ft. However, the project was really beyond the technical capability of those involved, and after a fire the scheme was abandoned. As a contemporary involved put it: 'Total cost of the well!! £15,242 10*s* 4¼*d*' – an enormous sum at this time. *(AC)*

The latest answer to crossing the Thames – the QE II bridge seen from mid-river. *(BE)*

Buses travelled up Grays High Street in the 1950s. Pedestrianisation and traffic calming were unheard of in those days. *(AC)*

The pedestrianised High Street today. *(BE)*

London's wonderful buses made by AEC at Southall are represented here by STL 2689 on route 323A in Orsett Road in the 1960s. Buses now travel along Orsett Road only in the opposite direction and are poor substitutes for the AEC's smooth-riding vehicles of forty years ago. *(AC)*

The brand new bus station at Grays is one improvement in 2002. There is now a multiplicity of bus companies serving Thurrock. *(BE)*

Defence of the Realm

Some defence works have proved their worth over more than a century. This is Coalhouse Fort and the extra Second World War fortification built on top of the original massive works of the 1860s is clearly visible. The Thames has always been a key to Britain's defences. The Vikings and Dutch were just two of the invaders who passed along it with impunity. German aerial bombers used its silver ribbon to guide them to London in two world wars. *(KL)*

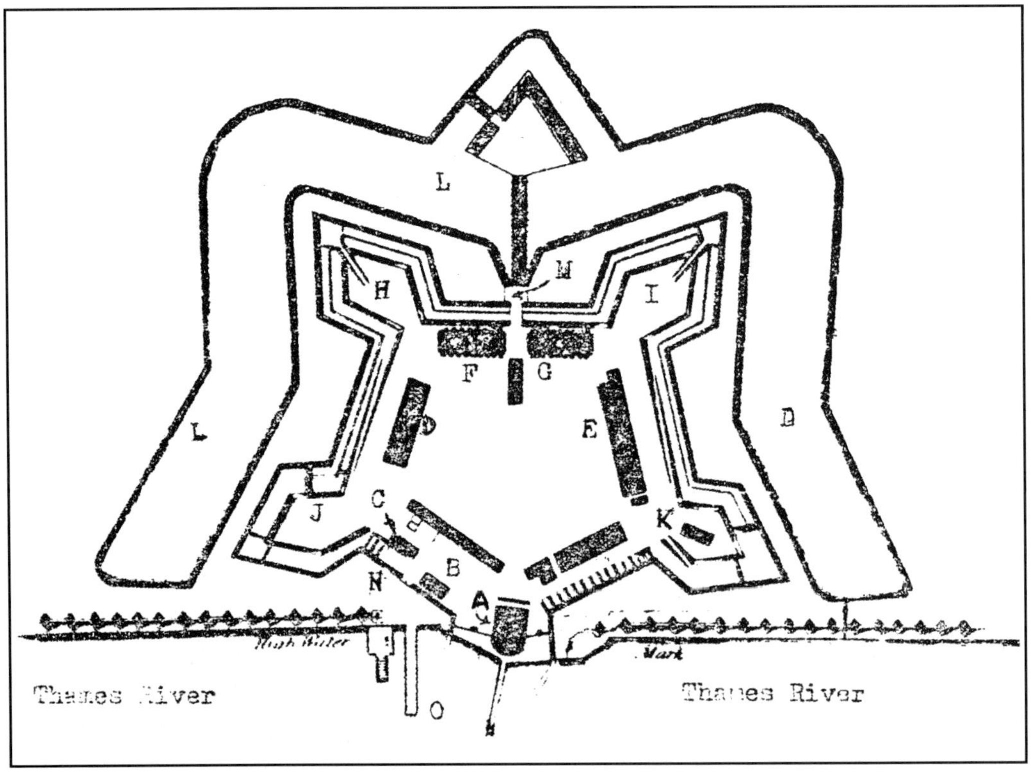

Tilbury Fort defences, 1725. The original fort was a masterpiece of seventeenth-century military engineering created by Sir Bernard de Gomme, Charles II's chief engineer. A smaller predecessor had been constructed during Henry VIII's reign and afterwards modified during the crisis times of the Armada years. *(AC)*

A view of Tilbury Fort from the river, 1808. In 1860 the Thames estuary defences were reorganised and an effort was made to bring the fort up to date. Further improvements were made up to the end of the Second World War and it was continuously garrisoned to this time. English Heritage now look after it and it is open to the public. *(AC)*

The entrance and forward bastion of Coalhouse Fort. Throughout the eighteenth and first half of the nineteenth centuries Tilbury and Gravesend batteries were the first line of defence for the Thames and London. However, in 1795 forward batteries were put in at Coalhouse Point, Hope Point and Shornmead. In the 1840s and 1850s those at Coalhouse Point and Shornmead were replaced by earthen batteries for seventeen and thirteen guns respectively. Then came the report of 1860, a bombshell which found the existing defences inadequate to protect the vital targets that lay up the Thames – Purfleet powder magazine, Woolwich Arsenal, merchant shipping and London itself. Very soon large, strong forts began to be constructed at Coalhouse, Shornmead and Cliffe Creek – large casemated batteries of more than twenty guns. *(KL)*

& CREDIT
FURNISHER

Volunteers from Grays and district, High Street, Grays, *c.* 1914. Huge crowds turned out at Grays to see off recruits to the titanic battles of the First World War. A policeman and boy bandsmen led the marching men to the waiting trains. They were soon to be posted to training camps and then to the fields of France or naval operations. *(TMS)*

The Zeeland Steamship Compar
at Tilbury with exchange
VLISSINGEN
PRINSE
Dampfer „Prinses Juliana" der Dampfs
in Tilbury mit ausgetauschten v

Steamship *Prinses Juliana* sails into Tilbury for an exchange of wounded prisoners, First World War. *(AC)*

Many women moved into industrial work to help the war effort. Nitro explosives, gunpowder and cordite had been made at Kynoch's factory on the marshes since the late nineteenth century. Now it was vital to the Allied war effort that women filled the gaps left by the men who had gone to the front. *(TMS)*

How did they find time for football? These young girls, many of them from as far off as Barking, Southend, Billericay and Pitsea, worked long shifts of twelve hours then had to make difficult journeys to and fro. They were collected by horse brakes from Stanford-le-Hope station and taken the 5 miles to the munition works on the lonely marshes. But team spirit drove them on and two women's football teams – 'A' shift and 'B' shift – were established. They even trained twice a week in an era when few women took part in sport. *(AC)*

This photograph of a Zeppelin passing over Tilbury on a raid was snapped from a back garden during the First World War. *(TMS)*

"OUR BOYS BROUGHT DOWN ZEPPELIN L15."

Thames Villagers' Story Of A Wonderful Night.

HIT SEVERAL TIMES.

"The Whole Gun Crew Did It—Everybody Helping."

IDOLISED CAPTAIN.

Got Out Of Sick-Bed To Take Charge, Wrapped In A Blanket.

[The first account of the winning hit, or hits, at L15 from the gun-crew in a Thames village is told in the following exclusive narrative.]

From Our Special Correspondent.

SOMEWHERE IN ESSEX, Sunday.

If the Censor would allow me to tell the full story of how the Zeppelin was brought down, and the men who did it, the country would be ringing with admiration for a group of men who were directly responsible for the success.

But this is too much to hope, and therefore we must leave names and places to the imagination of the public.

The little village of —— is en fête to-day.

If you ask why there are so many smiles and the sound of hearty laughter on all sides, you will be met with: "Why, haven't you heard? Our boys brought the Zeppelin down."

It is common gossip in this snug little village of the Thames and they are very proud and justly so.

"THATS THE GUN."

"That's the gun that did it," they say, excitedly, pointing to the gun that has for many days been the great local attraction.

Almost all the villagers saw the Zeppelin, and saw it hit twice.

Inquiries I had made at towns within a radius of twelve miles confirmed the villagers' and

This cap was picked up in a field in one of the raided areas. It is believed to have been dropped by one of the Zeppelin's crew.

soldiers' story that the big —— gun "did the trick."

To-day I have spoken to one or two of the gun crew at ——, and they, together with men of other gun crews, were unanimous that the gun was responsible.

"We received the alarm," said a bombardier who was serving a gun near, "about nine o'clock. In less than three minutes we were at our post and ready to fire.

"We picked the 'Zepp' up about 9.45 p.m., flying at about 15,000 feet, and coming over from the north-east.

"Naturally we started to fire right away—before the searchlights had even picked her up. But we didn't hit her, although we got perilously near.

"Very soon after we started the gun at —— got busy, and the searchlights too.

"It was a grand sight. She was lighted up like a silver cigar, and we could see the shells bursting all round her.

CAUGHT IN THE STERN.

"Presently a shot from the gun caught the Zepp. in the stern, and a little flame shot out from the envelope, whether from our bursting shell or the ballonette I couldn't tell from our position. Anyhow, the explosion seemed to throw it round, and at the same time it dropped by the stern with nose in the air.

"Of course, we were busy with our gun, but the boys couldn't help making a slight pause to shout 'She's hit.' And then we were busy again. But the next shot caught her again near the bow towards the centre, and that seemed to paralyse the monster, for she appeared to remain stationary for a couple of seconds before continuing her flight slowly to north and out of range.

"We knew that she had been very badly hit, and we were all confident that she must drop sooner or later.

"Our only regret was that our gun wasn't responsible. Still, we don't mind so much, because they were gunners of our regiment that did bring her down."

Later I met and conversed with another gunner, who told me the story of the gun's success

"We brought her down all right; anyone will tell you that for miles around," he replied, with conviction, to my question.

In answer to my query, Who was the man? he replied, "One man is not responsible for it. The whole gun-crew did it. If anyone is responsible at all it is Captain ——, who was in charge and secured the range.

"Every man has something to do, and if he fails he delays or upsets the firing.

"But Captain —— is a marvel!"

IN A BLANKET.

Then the Bombardier explained that the Captain in charge of the gun has been, and still is, ill. On Friday, by the doctor's orders, he was in bed. When he heard of the alarm, without a moment's hesitation he left his bed, dressed and, wrapping himself in a large blanket, went straight to his gun to take command.

There is no doubt that the Captain is idolised by his men, and two or three of them said with pride: "The Captain loves the gun, and would never leave if if he had his way."

How well the Captain succeeded has already been told.

One of his gunners, in conversation with me, said:—"The Captain gave us the orders, and we fired. The first shot was too short, the second and the third were too high, but with wonderful quickness the Captain soon found the range, and when we did hit the target it went through the stern and swung her back on her course, which was straight for London.

"When we landed one, it was easy to get another in, and we did, near the bow. But the first one was enough. We didn't see her drop, but we knew she was hurt and not likely to get across the water again.

FIRST SHOT SMASHED THE RUDDER.

'The first shot must have smashed her rudder wires, for she seemed to be going away in the direction in which our first shell turned her—to the north."

I put it to the gunners that others had claimed the distinction of bringing the Zeppelin down. But they quickly disposed of other claims by saying, "Why, the guns at —— and —— were too far away, and they were falling short.

"We hit our Zeppelin about ten o'clock, and she left in a very distressed state, with her nose in the air and throwing out bombs—not to do any particular damage, but as ballast. That is why you will find nine bomb holes at —— in the meadows."

TERRITORIAL GUNNERS.

The men responsible—I hope the Censor will let me say it—for hitting the Zeppelin are Territorials.

This roughly pasted up newspaper extract was proudly retained by locals who played a part in bringing down raiding airship L15 on 31 March 1916. A member of the Purfleet gun team, one of the many crews involved in shooting down the enemy airship, told how he and his colleague received a warning at 9 pm one night that Zeppelins were heading towards the battery and thereafter a sharp lookout was kept. The shape of the airship was seen high up in the sky at about 9.45, heading south-west. The team fired their guns immediately, only taking a few seconds to get the range. When a searchlight came on a shell was seen to strike the airship on the stern, then another in the bows. The vessel was hit repeatedly by the triangular battery before the Purfleet men lost sight of it. It crashed in the Thames and eighteen of the nineteen men aboard were rescued by trawlers. In total 353 service personnel involved in the action were awarded a gold medal with the words 'Well hit' and their names inscribed. *(AC)*

These pictures show the remnants of a Second World War anti-aircraft gun site on a farm in East Tilbury: *top*, the blockhouse; *middle*, underground armouries; *below*, circular mounting for gun. *(KL)*

Wartime spirit and humour is displayed by this group of civilians being given lessons in the use of a stirrup pump to tackle fires caused by incendiary bombs at Uplands Estate, Purfleet. *(TMS)*

The Bata factory Local Defence Volunteers (later known as the Home Guard) are drilled by George Noble (in uniform). Alf Estob, Ernie Shurben and Eric Purkiss are among those in the front row. *(TMS)*

In November 1940 there was a collection for the Thurrock Spitfire Fund outside Grays fire station, Orsett Road. *(TMS)*

The aftermath of a raid, Purfleet Road, Aveley, 13 March 1941. Mary Gower was killed at no. 98. The bungalows were later rebuilt. *(TMS)*

Thames Board Mills in-house magazine carried this dramatic shot of an observer on a rooftop in 1940. The observation posts to look out for approaching raiders were a welcome addition to a sophisticated TBM defence system involving eighty-four internal shelters for staff constructed out of 80,000 sandbags. There were also concrete shelters and other protected posts for key men and the Home Guard. Various squads were detailed for fire fighting, first aid, decontamination and rescue service. *(AC)*

Thurrock's guns are silenced now, but its illustrious record over the centuries is commemorated in the museum housed at the old Purfleet magazine. *(KL)*

Acknowledgements

Thanks are due to Keith Langridge for his excellent modern photographs, marked KL. Other pictures were supplied by Thurrock Museum Service (TMS); Thurrock Libraries Local Collection (TLS); Thames Board Mills (TBM); and the Osborne family (OF). Pictures marked AC are from the author's collection and those marked BE were taken by the author.

The plaque in the partly rebuilt tower at East Tilbury church erected by men of the London Electrical Engineers in 1917 in memory of those killed in the First World War. The tower had been destroyed by the Dutch in 1667. *(KL)*

ELECTRICAL
DISCOUNT
SPECIALISTS
Panasonic
Technics
CARPETS Tel. 01375 372341